Absolute Crime Presents:

You've Been Hacked

15 Hackers You Hope Your Computer Never
Meets

ABSOLUTE
CRIME

By William Webb

Absolute Crime Books

www.absolutecrime.com

Table of Contents

About Us

Absolute Crime publishes only the best true crime literature. Our focus is on the crimes that you've probably never heard of, but you are fascinated to read more about. With each engaging and gripping story, we try to let readers relive moments in history that some people have tried to forget.

Remember, our books are not meant for the faint at heart. We don't hold back—if a crime is bloody, we let the words splatter across the page so you can experience the crime in the most horrifying way!

If you enjoy this book, please visit our homepage to see other books we offer; if you have any feedback, we'd love to hear from you!

Hackers: A New Breed of Outlaw for a New World

Hackers have become one of the iconic symbols of our age. These new age outlaws have changed the way we view computers, technology, and our world. They have become heroes to many and symbols of a frightening new world to others.

Hackers redefined technology by demonstrating that giant computer networks could be used to empower the individual. Instead of making people nothing but cogs in the machine, computers enable those that can crack the code to manipulate the system for their own ends.

This power over technology makes hackers both romantic and frightening. Turning the tools of big government and big business against their creators makes hackers romantic outlaws. Individuals like Julian Assange and Samy Kamkar and groups like Anonymous try to portray themselves as modern-day Robin Hoods fighting tyranny and corruption.

Yet the same power over technology is frightening. Anybody anywhere can steal your most closely guarded secrets and your money through hacking. There is no privacy and no secrecy in cyberspace because of hackers. It's easy to see how and why hackers have captured the public imagination. They've changed the world and will keep changing it through the power of technology.

Australia's First Hacker: Nahshon Even-Chaim of the Realm

Nahshon Even-Chaim's career as a hacker is marked by a number of firsts. He was the first person convicted for cybercrimes in Australia. He was also one of the first hackers specifically targeted and brought down by a national police agency.

Even-Chaim was a true pioneer – he was hacking before most people had ever heard of the internet. Indeed, some of his activities predated the creation of the World Wide Web in 1989. Even-Chaim was also a leading member of one of the earliest hacking groups, the Realm, based in his hometown of Melbourne.

Hacking Before the Web

When Even-Chaim started hacking in the 1980s, there was no World Wide Web; instead, there were loose networks of computers at research institutions, universities, government agencies, and corporations. These computers communicated with each over the phone lines, but there was nothing like today's internet.

When Even-Chaim, who called himself Phoenix, started hacking, he had to physically dial the computers on the phone and connect via modem, although by 1990, the World Wide Web had been created and Even-Chaim was on it.

Phoenix's targets were what worried Australian authorities – his hacking targeted defense installations and research institutions. The Australian Federal Police (the equivalent of the American FBI) began investigating Even-Chaim for violating a new law that covered cybercrimes.

Caught by a Wiretap

The Federal Police had become aware of Even-Chaim's activities in 1988, possibly through an informant in the Realm. To catch him the police used an old but highly effective method – they got a warrant and tapped his telephone.

Investigators began monitoring Even-Chaim's phone on Jan. 26, 1990 and kept up the monitoring for eight weeks. They recorded Even-Chaim bragging and joking. Like many hackers, Even-Chaim was undone by his bravado. He bragged that he had been able to get into NASA's computers and hack local universities.

Even-Chaim and other Realm members apparently hacked into computers at universities in Melbourne. Those computers had a direct connection to NASA and other installations in the United States, which the Realm used to steal information.

Stealing Information Around the World

Even-Chaim was one of the first hackers to realize that he could steal information all over the world, not just in his own country. He was able to get into a NASA computer in Virginia (probably at the Langley Research Center), the University of California at Berkley, the Lawrence Livermore National Laboratory (a nuclear weapons facility in California), the University of Wisconsin at Madison, and into Purdue University's systems in Indiana.

Yet he was able to do this without leaving his home in Melbourne. It's easy to see why authorities were so worried. The crime was a new one and a frightening one. What's interesting to note is the motivation for the data thefts is not clear.

The Realm members didn't try to sell the information, nor did they make use of it. They seemed to have acted for their own amusement and little else.

Hacking and Celebrity

Even-Chaim was also one of the first celebrity hackers. He phoned *The New York Times* and complained about an article that attributed his break-ins to somebody else. Even-Chaim was upset because the article had attributed his work to him.

On April 2, 1990, the Phoenix got all the attribution he could want – the Australian Police raided his home in the Melbourne suburb of Caulfield North. Two other Realm members, Richard Jones (or Electron) and David John Woodcock, who was known as Nom, were also picked up.

Nahshon Even-Chaim found himself facing 48 counts of computer crime and facing 10 years in jail. He ultimately pleaded guilty to 15 of the charges, and his sentence was reduced to 500 hours of community service and a 12-month suspended jail sentence.

Off the Radar

Even-Chaim has something else in common with other famous hackers – he quickly dropped from sight after his arrest and has stayed out of sight ever since. Like the famed hackers who came after him, the man once called Phoenix has gone out of his way to stay out of the limelight.

Even-Chaim has avoided publicity since his hacking days. Reports indicate that he worked at IT in Melbourne and he may have been involved in the local music scene. Since his downfall, Even-Chaim has avoided all requests for interviews. He refused to cooperate with Kevin Anderson, who produced a documentary about the Realm's activities called *In the Realm of the Hackers*.

The pioneering hacker is now more of a mystery than ever. His motives and his activities are still unknown and will probably remain a mystery.

Bibliography

Brisbane 2600. "Famous Hackers Nashon Even-Chaim." n.d. bris2600.com. Blog Entry. 28 May 2013.

Wikipedia. "Nashon Even-Chaim." n.d. en.wikipedia.org. Online Encyclopedia Entry. 28 May 2013.

From Whiz Kid to Super Hacker: Jerome Heckenkamp

Jerome Heckenkamp was a real life computer science prodigy whose life went far off track. In a few short weeks he went from working at one of America's top secret research installations, the Los Alamos National Laboratory, to sitting in a federal lock up on hacking charges.

Military Researcher by Day, Hacker by Night

At the time of his arrest for hacking, Heckenkamp was actually working in a secure area of Los Alamos as a computer network engineer. It isn't known if he was working on nuclear weapons or other classified military technology or not. Yet it is known what the young genius was doing in his spare time.

Even as he worked with classified military data by day, Heckenkamp was hacking the websites of major corporations at night. He reportedly did hundreds of thousands of dollars' worth of damage to such corporate giants as Qualcomm, Juniper Networks, E-Trade, and eBay from his dorm room. Ironically enough, the federal employee who presumably had a security clearance was eventually investigated and arrested by the FBI.

A Real Life Boy Genius

Jerome Heckenkamp was an authentic boy genius who began teaching himself algebra at age eight. The young man who was born in Australia but grew up in Wisconsin started college when he was 14 and graduated at age 18 when most students are completing high school.

Heckenkamp's double life had begun even before he graduated and started work at Los Alamos—the place where the atomic bomb was invented. He had already started hacking into e-commerce companies' websites from his dorm room at the University of Wisconsin at Madison.

Jerome Heckenkamp started work at Los Alamos in 1999. By then Heckenkamp was also a liar; he falsely claimed to have a master's degree in computer science from the University of Wisconsin. Despite the lack of a degree, Heckenkamp was asked to lecture on computer programming at the University of New Mexico.

The Hacker Gets Hacked

Authorities became aware of Heckenkamp's activities in December 1999, when somebody attempted a cyber-attack on the semiconductor company Qualcomm. Qualcomm's security experts notified the FBI, which was able to track the attack back to a server at the University of Wisconsin. The feds alerted the University's systems administrator, Jeffrey Savoy, who launched an investigation of his own.

Savoy managed to trace the source of the attack to Heckenkamp's dorm room computer. Savoy also discovered that Heckenkamp was trying to hack the University's e-mail system.

Since he was unable to block the attack, Savoy decided to do some hacking of his own on Heckenkamp's computer. He cracked Savoy's computer and made an interesting discovery. Heckenkamp had a secret identity; he was a famous hacker nicknamed MagicFX. MagicFX had been brazen enough to deface eBay's website and brag about it to *Forbes* magazine.

The Hacker in Court

Savoy immediately contacted the FBI, which got a warrant and seized Heckenkamp's computer in New Mexico. Once agents searched the Linux machine, they got enough evidence to file charges against the young genius.

When he appeared in court in January 2001, Heckenkamp found himself facing up to 85 years in prison and $14 million in fines. Federal prosecutors alleged that Heckenkamp had been able to gain root access to UNIX systems at big companies through the University of Wisconsin's network. He was familiar with the network because the hacker had once worked at the University's computer help desk.

Heckenkamp was arrested in New Mexico; he was fired from his job at Los Alamos as soon as officials there found out about his hacking activities. Interestingly enough, the man who was accused of causing $1 million worth of damage to various large companies had to stay in jail because he didn't have the funds to make bail.

Heckenkamp proved to be as adept in court as he was in cyberspace. He hired high profile cyber law attorney Jennifer Granick, who challenged the case. Granick tried to claim that the feds had violated the hacker's civil rights by searching his computer without a warrant. This would have made the evidence gathered inadmissible in court and forced the feds to withdraw the charges.

The Appeal Fails

The U.S. Ninth Circuit Court of Appeals eventually rejected Heckenkamp's argument in an important ruling that will affect many hacking cases. The court found that Savoy had not broken the law and had not been acting as an agent of the FBI when he searched Heckenkamp's computer. That meant the federal case against Heckenkamp would stand.

Heckenkamp pleaded guilty and was sentenced to time served, which was eight months in jai. It isn't clear what Heckenkamp is doing today or where he is. The man once described as a super hacker has dropped completely from sight.

Interestingly enough, the boy genius still claims that he is innocent. Heckenkamp insists that he was set up by unknown parties. He has never said who framed him or why; instead he simply says he's innocent. Since he pled guilty to the charges, it is hard to take these claims seriously. The man who started out as a genius ended up sounding and acting like any common criminal.

Bibliography

Associated Press. "Suspected Hacker Jailed After Failing to Post Bail." 9 February 2001. articles.latimes.com. Wire Service News Article. 29 May 2013.

Clark, Heather. "Los Alamos Employee Denies Hacking." 12 January 2001. abcnews.go.com. ABC News Article. 29 May 2013.

Poulsen, Kevin. "Court Okays Counter-Hack eBay Hacker's Computer (Updated)." 6 April 2007. wired.com. Wired News Article. 29 May 2013.

Wikipedia. "Jerome Heckenkamp." n.d. en.wikipedia.org. Online Encyclopedia Entry. 29 May 2013.

Hacking the International Space Station: Jonathan James

Jonathan James' life was short, but notable, and even though he died young, James earned fame as the man who hacked the International Space Station when he was just 15 years old. James' other targets included the U.S. Department of Defense, the top secret U.S. Defense Threat Reduction Agency, and NASA.

U.S. authorities considered James such a threat to national defense that federal agents raided his home. James became a legendary hacker, yet his life became a cautionary tale for hackers. The glory he earned for his early exploits led to tragedy and a sad early death.

Just seven years after hacking NASA, James was accused of attacking retailers and stealing money. Less than a year after his second arrest, James was dead. He killed himself rather than go to prison. Worst of all, there is some evidence that James might have been innocent of the second series of cyber-attacks. He might have been framed by other hackers.

Hacking NASA

Jonathan James' story is actually a rather tragic one. He went from hero-worshipping U.S. astronauts to being placed under arrest by NASA agents. When he was a boy, James kept an autographed picture of his favorite astronaut, Mike Coats, next to his bed. The inscription on the photograph said: "Dare to Dream." Unfortunately, James dared to dream, but in a very different way.

James was a second-generation computer geek. His father, Robert, was a computer programmer. Robert later told reporters that he was proud of some of what Jonathan had accomplished.

James decided to see if he could learn more about spaceflight by hacking into NASA facilities, including the Marshall Space Flight Center in Huntsville, Ala. Using the handle "Comrade", James was able to steal the environmental control software for the International Space Station. That meant that James could have theoretically raised or lowered the temperature on the station.

James' other targets included the Defense Threat Reduction Agency (or DTRA), a top-secret department of the Pentagon responsible for defending America from weapons of mass destruction. The DTRA's mission includes treaty compliance and the dismantling of nuclear weapons in the former Soviet Union. James allegedly stole DTRA passwords and intercepted 3,000 messages passing through DTRA's email system. He got into DTRA through a backdoor server in Dulles, Va.

A Cyber Juvenile Delinquent

Not surprisingly, James' intrusion into such a top-secret network didn't go unnoticed. Cyber security experts were able to trace the calls James was making to NASA computers from the dialup modem in his family's home. Once they knew the number, the federal agents could trace the phone number to its source.

Agents from NASA and the Department of Defense stormed the James family's Miami-area home at 6 a.m. on Jan. 26, 2000. The agents took Jonathan into custody and confiscated the family computer.

Interestingly enough, James was charged with just counts of juvenile delinquency because of his age. James was placed under house arrest and probation until he left high school. At the time of his sentencing in September 2000, a U.S. attorney told the press that had James been an adult, he could have faced charges that would have brought him up to 10 years in prison.

From Hacking NASA to Hacking OfficeMax

Like many people who get ensnared in the criminal justice system, Jonathan James went from juvenile delinquent to hardcore criminal behind bars. Jonathan violated his probation by taking drugs and was sent to a federal juvenile facility in Alabama. After his return, James reportedly got caught up in a gang run by another notorious hacker named Albert Gonzalez.

By 2003, when he was 18, James was reportedly wardriving, or hacking wireless networks to steal credit card information from stores. By the time he was 24 James was facing serious criminal charges for a hacking scheme. Gonzalez, the ringleader, allegedly got away with tens of millions of dollars stolen from retailers. Secret Service agents called the scheme the largest identity theft ring in U.S. history.

The targets in Gonzalez's scheme were more down to earth than NASA and the International Space Station. The victims included the TJX department store chain, BJ's Wholesale Club, Boston Market, the Barnes & Noble bookstores, Sports Authority, the Forever 21 clothing stores, OfficeMax, and Dave & Buster's, a popular sports bar franchise. James was no longer a lone wolf – he was part of a ring of criminals that supposedly included 13 hackers. It isn't clear how federal authorities found the ring or linked James to it.

Death of a Hacker

Jonathan James shot himself at his brother's condo in Miami on May 18, 2008, a year after the Secret Service had arrested him for hacking. Secret Service agents were allegedly following James and had placed a tracking device on his car.

James left a five-page suicide note in which he claimed that he had been entrapped by federal authorities. James believed that he had been set up and betrayed by Albert Gonzalez, who was allegedly an informant for the Secret Service. In his note, James said he had no faith in the criminal justice system and felt he would be convicted for crimes he didn't commit.

At the time of his death, James apparently had no job and had never been to college. All he was apparently doing was living in a house he had inherited from his mother and hacking. The dream Jonathan James had dared to have had become a nightmare.

Bibliography

Poulsen, Kevin. "Former Teen Hacker's Suicide Lined to TJX Probe." 9 July 2009. wired.com. Wired Feature Article. 29 May 2013.

Stout, David. "Youth Sentenced in Government Hacking Case." 23 September 2000. nytimes.com. New York Times News Article. 29 May 2013.

Wikipedia. "Defense Threat Reduction Agency." n.d. en.wikipedia.org. Online Encyclopedia Entry. 29 May 2013.

—. "Jonathan James." n.d. en.wikipedia.org. Online Encyclopedia Entry. 29 May 2013.

Homeless Hacker and Snitch: Adrian Lamo

In a world full of strange and eccentric people – that of hackers, Adrian Lamo stands out as the oddest of the lot. At one time he was hacking into some of the world's largest companies' most secure networks and living in abandoned buildings because he had no job and no money.

Instead of bragging about his hacks on discussion boards or hatching schemes to steal millions, Lamo often politely told system administrators how he had violated their security. Some of the executives at companies he had victimized even praised Lamo as a hero. Other victims have pressed charges against Lamo for his actions, yet a lot of hackers condemned him as a fraud and a showoff.

Adrian Lamo always seems to generate opinions and controversy no matter what he does. In his most controversial move, Lamo became a villain to a lot of hackers and political activists when he helped military authorities locate and arrest cyber whistleblower and U.S. army enlisted man Bradley Manning, who had become a folk hero to many by turning 260,000 classified U.S. government documents over to the controversial website Wikileaks.

Hacker without a Home

The most unusual thing about Adrian Lamo is that he doesn't have a home. At different times, he's lived in his parents' house, on friends' couches, in abandoned buildings, and even in a mental hospital. Lamo admits that at many times in his life, the only thing he owned was his laptop. He travelled around the United States on the cheapest form of transportation possible, Greyhound buses, never staying in one place for more than a few days.

Unlike many hackers, Lamo has been very open and public about his life. He has talked often with the media and regularly revealed details about his personal life to reporters. Lamo even went on TV and demonstrated hacking techniques, something that enraged fellow crackers. Lamo's behavior has been erratic at times – he has cooperated with authorities and also expressed paranoid fears of the U.S. government.

Lamo is of Colombian descent – he was born in Boston and currently lives in California. In 2010, Lamo was put into a mental hospital for evaluation and diagnosed with Asperger's Syndrome, an autistic disorder that can create antisocial and odd behavior. Lamo has since publicly admitted he has the syndrome and mentioned it to reporters.

Hacking for Fun

Curiosity seems to be the main thing that drives Adrian Lamo – he says he is fascinated by dark and secret places like caves and sewers. Lamo apparently sees secured servers and encrypted data as the online equivalent of these and likes to break into them.

Lamo's first recorded hack occurred when he was 20. He hacked into Yahoo's news section and inserted a false quote he attributed to then-Attorney General John Ashcroft into a news story. After that, he went after several major sites, including Excite@Home, where he discovered a hole in the security.

Lamo's most brazen move got him into big trouble – he cracked *The New York Times*' network and stole a variety of information. The things stolen included the phone numbers of high profile contributors to the paper's Op-Ed page, including Warren Beatty and Rush Limbaugh. Interestingly enough, Lamo did nothing with the information – he simply stole it.

The Times didn't take Lamo's intrusion very lightly – it brought charges against him. Lamo went on the run, but then surrendered to federal authorities and pleaded guilty. He received six months detention at his parents' home and two years of probation.

Very Odd Behavior

Two very odd incidents happened to Lamo in
2010. He was arrested in California in May after
behaving oddly while filing a police report. That
led to the psychiatric evaluation and the
Asperger's diagnosis. He ended up in the
Woodland Memorial Hospital near Sacramento
and gave an interview about his experience to
Wired magazine writer Kevin Poulsen.

Later that year, Lamo was contacted by U.S.
Army Specialist Bradley Manning. Manning's job
in the army gave him access to classified
communications; Manning was troubled by the
contents of some of the communications and
wanted to make them public. Manning contacted
Lamo because he was impressed by a profile of
Lamo he had seen in *Wired*. At the time, Lamo
had been identified as a supporter of WikiLeaks.

Instead of helping Manning, Lamo notified the Army about Manning's claims. The Army then arrested Manning and placed him in a maximum security prison. This action, which could be seen as patriotic by some, was heavily criticized by hackers and admirers of WikiLeaks. Many of them condemned Lamo as a snitch and a traitor.

Hacker or Informant

Part of the reason why WikiLeaks admirers were so angry at Lamo were claims that Adrian Lamo was part of Project Vigilant, a top secret government program run by the FBI and the National Security Agency (NSA). The purpose of Project Vigilant is to use hackers and other volunteers to track down cyber criminals and security threats.

A *Forbes* magazine article named Lamo as one of the volunteers who works with Project Vigilant. One of Vigilant's missions was to find the source of diplomatic cables leaked to WikiLeaks.

Off the Grid Again

Adrian Lamo is currently in hiding because he has been threatened by Wikileaks supporters, who include radical anarchists and libertarians. He has been threatened by the cyber anarchist group Anonymous among others. Lamo's current whereabouts are unknown, but he's probably wandering the country with his laptop and still living the lifestyle of a homeless hacker again. One thing is certain; Adrian Lamo will probably surface again and generate more publicity.

Even though he's an antisocial loner, Adrian Lamo craves celebrity and the publicity it brings. That will probably lure him back out of the shadows at some point.

Bibliography

Greenberg, Andy. "Stealthy Government Contractor Monitors U.S. Internet Providers, Worked With Wikileaks Informant." 1 August 2010. forbes.com. Forbes Blog. 30 May 2013.

Pilkington, Ed. "Adrian Lamo on Bradley Manning: 'I knew my actions might cost him his life'." 3 January 2013. guardian.co.uk. Guardian Interview. 30 May 2013.

Poulsen, Kevin. "Ex-Hacker Adrian Lamo Institutionalized, Diagnosed with Asperger's." 20 May 2010. wired.com. Wired Feature Article. 30 May 2013.

Shachtman, Noah. "He Hacks by Day, Squats by Night." 2 June 2003. wired.com. Wired Feature Article. 30 May 2013.

Wikipedia. "Adrian Lamo." n.d. en.wikipedia.org. Online Encyclopedia Entry. 30 May 2013.

"MafiaBoy" Mike Calce: the Prince of Hackers

If there is a hacker who fits all the popular stereotypes, it is Michael Demon Calce, the man known as "MafiaBoy." As a high school student, Calce engineered successful cyber-attacks against several of the world's largest companies. His activities were so destructive that they reportedly prompted then-U.S. President Bill Clinton to call one of the first White House conferences on cyber security.

Calce wasn't old enough to drive when he became a hacking legend. He was just 15 years old when he took down some of the biggest sites on the web with denial of service attacks. His targets included CNN, Yahoo! (then the world's biggest search engine), eBay, and E*TRADE. Calce's technique was simple, but highly effective: he simply flooded the websites with so many false requests that he caused their servers to crash.

It is easy to see why Calce became a legend – he was a junk food eating teenager who lived with his mother when he became famous. Yet at one point, U.S. Attorney General Janet Reno actually vowed to devote all of the U.S. Justice Department's resources to bringing MafiaBoy (Calce's alias in chat rooms) to justice.

He Grew Up With the Internet

Mike Calce grew up with the internet. He was born in the mid-1980s and received his first computer at the age of six (around 1991) when the net first appeared. Calce was part of the first generation to grow up with the net. Like some hackers and legitimate computer geniuses, Calce turned to cyberspace for solace because of his terrible reality. Calce's parents were divorced and he was lonely and picked on at school, so he began spending all of his time online.

Calce's famed hacking exploits started as a dare when he was 15. A friend claimed that Calce could not hack CNN's website, but the teen rose to the challenge and took down the news site in a few minutes. The Montreal teenager was on his way to fame, if not fortune.

In February 2000, Calce decided to launch what he called "Project Rivolta" ("rivolta" is the Italian word for riot), a series of massive denial of service attacks on large corporate websites. The motivation for the attacks was apparently just to demonstrate his power and skills.

Teenaged Prank Shocks the World

Calce committed a teenaged prank designed to show off and impress his friends, mostly the members of his hacker group TNT. He thought he could establish dominance for TNT by abusing the file-sharing software Hotline. The strategy he used was a fairly simply one; Hotline would collect thousands of addresses, then launch automatic attacks from them.

Calce launched his offensive on Feb. 7, 2000 by unleashing a series of massive denial of service attacks against giant e-commerce sites, including buy.com, Yahoo, Amazon.com, eBay, and Dell. The strategy he used was simple – bombard the company's server with so many requests that it would collapse – and it worked, because buy.com was shut down completely.

The attacks were automated: Calce would launch them and then head off for school. The boy who was turning the internet upside down was afraid to skip class, and didn't realize how much havoc he was wreaking.

$1.5 Billion in Damages

The attacks that MafiaBoy unleashed caused a vast amount of damage. Industry analyst Michael Kovar told reporters that the attacks caused $1.5 billion in damages. The Royal Canadian Mounted Police (RCMP), or the Mounties, later confirmed the figure, but the $1.5 billion damage claim has been disputed by historians.

His demonstration of the internet's vulnerability came at the right time. The Y2K hysteria, the belief that all computers would crash on Jan. 1, 2000 due to a software glitch, was still fresh in memory. The dot.com bubble was at its height in the financial markets, as gullible investors paid far too much for any net-related stock.

Authorities mobilized and began searching for the source of the attacks. FBI and RCMP agents began checking hacker bulletin boards to see if they could learn anything. They noticed that somebody who called himself Mafiaboy had inside knowledge of the attacks and was bragging about it. Cyber sleuths began trying to track him down in the real world.

Boasting Led to Arrest

The RCMP was able to bag MafiaBoy fairly quickly because hackers liked to brag about their exploits. Cybercrime experts noticed that Mafiaboy knew exactly how the attacks were launched and what applications were used.

When the Mounties arrived at Calce's father's condo, the teenager was reportedly eating junk food and bragging to friends. The young man was confused and didn't realize what he had done or the extent of his activities.

Interestingly enough, Mafiaboy never spent any time behind bars. Instead he pleaded guilty to 56 hacking related charges and was sentenced to eight months at a home for juvenile offenders and a year of probation. The judge put restraints on him that restricted his computer use to the machines at his school.

Mafia Boy Doesn't Like Modern Hackers

Now grown up, Mafia Boy has reinvented himself as a minor celebrity and cyber security expert. He gives interviews, once wrote a column on cyber security for a Montreal newspaper, and wrote an autobiography called *Mafiaboy: How I Cracked the Internet and Why It's Still Broken* with a ghostwriter.

Calce has also spoken out against today's hackers – he seems to see them as greedy and simplistic. Calce gets particularly upset when he is compared to hackers that download tools online. Those individuals are not real hackers because it is too easy to get away with such crimes today.

The former Mafiaboy is disgusted by the greed of criminal hackers and seems to admire politically motivated hactivists like Anonymous and Luzsec. In the ultimate shift, Calce now gives average people security advice, such as installing firewalls and using stronger passwords. The formerly famous hacker also advises people not to use Wi-Fi and Facebook because those technologies are too vulnerable to hacking.

Bibliography

Gross, Doug. "'Mafiaboy' breaks silence, paints 'portrait of a hacker'." 15 August 2011. cnn.com. CNN Interview. 28 May 2013.

Hopper, D. Ian. "Canadian teen charged in Web site attack released." 19 April 2000. archives.cnn.com. CNN News Article. 28 May 2013.

Pachal, Pete. "Former Hacker: Today's Hacks Are All About the Money." 15 August 2012. mashabale.com. Mashable Feature Article. 28 May 2013.

Wikipedia. "MafiaBoy." n.d. en.wikipedia.org. Online Encyclopedia Entry. 28 May 2013.

Maksym Yastremskiy: A Cyber Crime Kingpin

The Internet's biggest attractions are anonymity and connectivity; the ability to reach out and connect with others all over the world yet remain anonymous while doing so. One hacker that took advantage of these traits in a big way was Maksym Yastremskiy, the man known as Maksik.

We don't know that much about Yastremskiy except that he comes from the Ukraine, part of the former Soviet Union. Yet this shadowy figure was involved in one of the biggest cybercrimes in history: the theft of 180 million credit and debit card numbers from U.S. retailers between 2004 and 2008. The interesting thing is that crime was only one of many activities in which a man described as a cyber-crime kingpin was supposedly involved.

Yastremiskiy made history as one of the first cyber fences; he made a fortune by selling information stolen by hackers to other hackers. The Ukrainian was supposedly at the center of a multinational racket that was bringing in millions of dollars, yet he didn't even know the names of some of his closest associates. Maksik also managed to steal from tens of millions of Americans, including some of America's largest companies, without setting foot in the United States.

Providing a Market for the Hackers

Maksym Yastremskiy was both a hacker and a middleman, who arranged black-market deals for other criminals. He was able to get away with this because he lived and worked in the Ukraine. The Ukraine did not have an extradition treaty with the U.S., so Maksik felt safe from U.S. authorities.

Even though U.S. law enforcement agencies, including the Secret Service, were aware of his activities, they couldn't touch him unless he made the mistake of traveling to a country with an extradition treaty to the U.S.

Yastremiskiy's most famous deal was with the notorious American hacker, Albert Gonzalez, who was masterminding the large-scale theft of credit card numbers from big U.S. retailers. Gonzalez planted malware in the retailers' computer systems that captured credit card numbers and transmitted it to him. He then sold the numbers and other information to Yastremiskiy, who sold it to other crooks.

Your Credit Card Information for Sale Cheap

It isn't known how much Yastremiskiy paid for each of the credit card numbers, but he reportedly made $11 million off the deal for the years 2004–2006 alone. Nor is it known how Yastremiskiy and Gonzalez hooked up. Gonzalez was involved in Shadowcrew.com, an online community for hackers and other cyber crooks that had members around the world.

During its heyday in the early 2000s, Shadowcrew served as a sort of social media network and market for hackers. Crooks would gather and make deals. Gonzalez, who was working as an informant for the Secret Service at the time, would troll the site looking for crooks to turn in. He was also apparently recruiting henchmen for his massive cyber fraud scheme.

He and Maksik apparently met there and went into business. Interestingly enough, Maksik only knew Gonzalez through his screen name, Segvec. Maksik knew nothing about Gonzalez except that he could help him make a lot of money.

Spy Games

The Secret Service reportedly made contact with Maksik through an undercover agent, who bought credit data from him. The agent was even able to meet Maksik in Dubai, and in a scene out of a spy movie, hack the hacker's laptop. The Secret Service didn't get enough to arrest the man, but they were able to track him.

The real lucky break came in 2007, when Maksik made the mistake of going to Turkey and trying to hack at least 12 banks in that country. Turkish police caught Maksik at a nightclub in the beach resort town of Kemer.

It isn't known how Turkish police were able to locate Yastremiskiy; the most likely scenario is that the Secret Service tipped them off to his location. Once he was in custody, Turkish authorities let American agents search his laptop. The agents found a treasure trove of information, including instant messages between Maksik and Segvec that would eventually enable them to connect Gonzalez to the conspiracy.

Cracking the Encryption with a Rubber Hose

Turkish police may have resorted to some old and very inhumane methods to get Maksik to talk and reveal the keys to his encryption software to them. Some news reports indicate that Yastremiskiy might have been tortured or threatened with torture to get him to confess.

The allegations are based on a joke supposedly made by a U.S. Justice Department official named Howard Cox. Cox reportedly told a conference of federal law enforcement officials that the best way to get a suspect to talk was to leave him alone with the Turkish police for a week. He even told the attendees Maksik's passwords.

This method is called "rubber hose cryptanalysis" after the old police tactic of beating suspects with a rubber hose. Rubber hoses were used because they don't leave any visible marks when used to beat somebody. It is morally repugnant, but it apparently works. These allegations were denied by the Turkish Embassy in Washington, which issued a press release that noted that medical examinations found no sign of physical harm on Yastremiskiy's body.

Still an Enigma

We still don't know that much about Maksik, but we know where he will be for the next 30 years: in a Turkish prison. In January 2009 a court in Turkey sentenced Yastremiskiy to 30 years in prison for hacking local banks. The court also fined the hacker $23,200, which is probably chump change to him. The U.S. Department of Justice has tried to get Yastremiskiy extradited to the United States; there is no sign Turkish courts would go along with such a move, so he will probably stay in Turkey.

Maskym Yastremiskiy's career proves that it is now possible for criminals, like everybody else, to do business anywhere in the world. His career also demonstrates that it is a good idea for professional criminals to stay out of Turkey.

Bibliography

Dunn, John E. "TJX hacker banged up for 30 years." 8 January 2009. news.techworld.com. Techworld News Article. 30 May 2013.

Leyden, John. "Carder linked to TJX hack jailed for 30 years by Turkish court." 8 January 2009. theregister.co.uk. Register News Article. 30 May 2013.

Poulsen, Kevin. "Hacking Godfather 'Maksik' Sentenced to 30 years by Turkish Court." 8 January 2009. wired.com. Wired News Article. 30 May 2013.

Soghoian, Chris. "Turkish police may have beaten encryption key out of TJ Maxx suspect." 27 January 2009. news.cnet.com. CNET News Commentary. 30 May 2013.

Verini, James. "The Great Cyberheist." 10
November 2010. nytimes.com. New York Times
Magazine Feature Article. 29 May 2013.

From Unix Terrorist to IT Professional to Keynote Speaker: Stephen Watt

No hacker has had a stranger journey through the world of cyberspace than Stephen Watt. Watt's life story reflects the strange history of hacking over the last 20 years – he went from teenaged rebel to highly paid software writer, criminal, and keynote speaker.

Watt's tale also reflects popular attitudes about hacking – the public first accepted hackers as popular heroes, rebels, and outlaws that flaunted the rules. The people against hackers discovered that many of them were criminals who preyed upon average folks. Watt, who was caught up in the hacker lifestyle, symbolized the uneasy relationship that society has with such geniuses.

Stephen Watt fits a few of the popular stereotypes of a hacker. He wears punk hairdos, likes to wear t-shirts with weird sayings on them, and has earrings. Yet he's also seven feet tall and has the body of an athlete. Unlike most computer nerds, Watt spends time at the gym and actually knows what weights are. A friend called him a weightlifting fiend. He looks more like a pro wrestler than a hacker. Unlike most hackers, you wouldn't want to run into Stephen Watt in a dark alley.

Project Mayhem

Like some other hackers, Stephen Watt was an authentic prodigy. He graduated high school when he was just 16 and completed college at age 19. Watt was a good dedicated student with a grade point average of 4.37, yet he had some interesting hobbies that showed some other aspects to his personality.

Calling himself the Unix Terrorist and Jim Jones (after the preacher-turned-Marxist cult leader who poisoned hundreds of followers in the 1970s), Watt was part of something called Project Mayhem. The project was a computer gang designed to making the lives of so-called "white-hat" hackers miserable. "White-hat" hackers were crackers who crossed the line and went to work as security experts.

Project Mayhem went out of its way to steal personal information about the white hats and spread it around the web. At the DefCon 2 hacker conference in 2002, Watt even walked onto the stage and showed the audience copies of messages he had hacked from white hat e-mail accounts.

A Hacker with Honor

Even though he liked to hack, Watt had a strong sense of honor and ethics. He refused to engage in criminal activities and viewed it as more of a game, although one of his online friends, a high school dropout named Albert Gonzalez, had other ideas. Gonzalez, whom Watt exchanged emails with, was already committing identity theft and credit card fraud.

After college, Watt went legitimate. He moved to New York and went to work at the Wall Street firm Morgan Stanley, earning $90,000 a year as a software engineer. He later worked at Imagine Software, earning $130,000 a year to develop real-time trading programs for financial firms, yet he was still participating in discussions and chats with hackers.

Undone by Friendship

Watt's taste of success on Wall Street ended because of his association with Gonzalez, who had become an informant for the Secret Service and the mastermind of one of the largest credit card fraud schemes in history. Gonzalez had become the leader of a hacker gang that had managed to crack databases at several large retailers, including OfficeMax, Target, and TJX (the parent company of TJ Maxx and Marshall's). The databases contained credit and debit card information, which they sold or used to take cash from ATMs.

Watt made the mistake of writing some code that Gonzalez used for a sniffer program. A sniffer was a worm that detected data from recent credit card transactions and sent them back to Gonzalez's computer. Gonzalez and his henchmen used a number of methods to insert such sniffers into the computer networks at large retailers. The sniffers may have stolen as many as 170 million credit and debit card numbers.

Watt wasn't involved in the ring, although he may have been aware of Gonzalez's activities. He attended a $75,000 birthday bash that Gonzalez threw for himself in Miami. At the time, Gonzalez was unemployed and had no job history, yet he was driving around town in a brand new BMW and staying at posh hotels.

Caught in the Net

Stephen Watt's world came crashing down on Aug. 13, 2008, when federal agents raided Imagine Software and arrested him. Watt didn't realize it, but the Secret Service had finally managed to connect Gonzalez to the identity theft ring and learned that Watt had written the code for the sniffer. It isn't exactly clear how agents connected Watt to the ring – he may have been ratted out by Gonzalez or one of his associates.

Gonzalez had made millions off the scam, and when he got caught, he had $1.5 million buried in his parents' backyard. His cohort in crime, Maksym Yastremski, a Ukrainian cyber fence, reportedly made $11 million selling the stolen credit card numbers. Stephen Watt got nothing and lost his job. He was fired as soon as the feds set foot at Imagine Software.

Watt was convicted of violating the Computer Fraud and Abuse Act and sentenced to two years in prison. A federal judge ordered him to pay $171.5 million in restitution for his role in Gonzalez's scheme. Watt went from living the good life on Wall Street to serving time in a minimum-security federal prison in Seattle with child pornographers and illegal immigrants.

The Unix Terrorist Cannot Pay the Rent

Today, Stephen Watt is broke. He and his wife live in an apartment in Florida that his mother pays for, and Watt is barred from working in the securities industry. He cannot use a computer unless it is monitored by the government. He can work as a web developer, but rarely makes enough to pay the bills because he cannot design securities software. Even though he has a hard time paying the bills, Watt has to pay 10% of his salary in restitution.

Watt occasionally makes waves and some extra cash by speaking at conferences, such as the Infiltrate offensive security conference in Miami, where he was the keynote speaker. He also gives the occasional statement to tech industry publications. Stephen Watt's story proves that hacking isn't all fun and games; instead, it can sometimes become a tragedy of Shakespearean proportions.

Bibliography

Koetsier, John. "Convicted hacker Stephen Watt on Aaron Swartz 'It's just not justice'." 17 January 2013. venturebeat.com. Column. 30 May 2013.

Phrack Inc. "Profile on the UNIX Terrorist." n.d. phrack.com. Webzine Interview with Stephen Watt. 30 May 2013.

Sias, Michael. "Stephen Watt, a.k.a. "The Unix Terrorist," to Keynote Infiltrate Con." 24 January 2013. prweb.com. Press Release. 30 May 2013.

Zetter, Kim. "Caught in the System, Ex-Hacker is stalked by His Past." 24 April 2013. wired.com. Wired Feature Article. 30 May 2013.

—. "Former Morgan Stanley Coder Gets 2 Years in Prison for TJX Hack." 22 December 2009. wired.com. Wired News Article. 30 May 2013.

—. "TJX Hacker Was Awash in Cash: His Penniless Coder Faces Prison." 18 June 2009. wired.com. Wired Feature Article. 30 May 2013.

The Blaster Jeffrey Lee Parson

There are some hackers whose activities are so destructive that they are actually prevented from accessing the internet again. One of these was Jeffrey Lee Parson, a.k.a. Teekid, the mastermind behind the computer worm known as the Blaster. The Blaster, which is also known as Lovsan, Lovesan, MSBlast, and Blaster.ban, infected thousands of computers that ran on Windows XP and Windows 2000, two of the most popular operating systems of all time.

The Blaster was designed to launch a denial of service attack against the world's largest software company and its most popular operating systems. Parson was apparently trying to send a "message" to Microsoft CEO Bill Gates, then the world's richest man. The message was a bizarre one, which would supposedly cause Windows to shut down and display messages.

Love You San!!

The first message Blaster was supposed to send out was:

I just want to say LOVE YOU SAN!!soo much.

The other was:

Billy gates why do you make this possible? Stop making money and fix your software!!

Parson was apparently one of many computer nerds who thought Windows and other Microsoft products were substandard and highly vulnerable to attack. He apparently set out to fix the problem by sending out a message that would shut down computers running Windows products.

You Can't Fight Microsoft

The Blaster first caught the world's attention on Aug. 11, 2003, when it started infecting and shutting down PCs. It was supposed to shut down Windows PCs between the dates of Aug. 15 and Dec. 31, 2003. At least three other versions of the virus were reportedly in existence.

Parson was caught because each infection sent signals back to a website called t33kid.com, which was registered in his name. The Blaster worm also contained a file called teekids.exe. Teekid was apparently Parson's online secret identity. Federal cyber sleuths and security experts from Microsoft followed the trail that Parson had left through servers in San Diego.

By Aug. 19, 2003, FBI and Secret Service agents were knocking on the door of the Parson family home in Hopkins, Min., a Minneapolis suburb. The agents arrested Parson and seized seven computers.

A Very Stupid Hacker

Observers described Parson, who was just 18 at the time, as a very stupid hacker who took few steps to cover his tracks. It was a fairly easy chore for Microsoft security to follow his trail and sic the Feds on him.

The fast-acting Feds might have prevented a much greater crime wave. When investigators searched his computers, agents discovered information about thousands of individuals' personal communications and finances. It isn't known what Parson was planning to do with that information.

The attack reportedly caused between $5 and $10 million worth of damage to Microsoft. Yet at the time of the attack, Parson had only around $3 in his savings account. He was so broke that a federal judge assigned him a public defender. It isn't clear if Parson regarded himself as a Robin Hood fighting for the little guy or if he was planning to steal from thousands of victims.

Was He a Fall Guy or a Mastermind?

Federal prosecutors alleged that Parson was a key figure in the Blaster attack, yet Parson told the NBC Today show that he was simply a fall guy. Parson claimed that he was spreading a worm that somebody else created. Interestingly enough, prosecutors admitted that Parson didn't write the worm.

Instead, they accused the high school student of spreading it. It sounds as if Parson may have been used by other hackers who were trying to steal information from Microsoft users.

Parson did admit that he had been spreading the worm and pleaded guilty to transmission of code in January 2005. He was sentenced to 18 months in a federal penitentiary. He was placed under a restraining order that kept him from using the internet or a computer.

Attacks Continue

Even though federal agents put an end to Jeffrey Lee Parson's hacking activities, the Blaster apparently lived on. Two other worms that had the same effect, creating an empty screen in Windows, appeared within a year. They were called Welchia and Sasser worms.

It isn't known if Parson's confederates were behind these worms or not. There are still a lot of questions about Parson and his activities. It isn't known where he got the worm or who wrote it, nor is it known if he was part of a network of hackers or not.

Some online reports indicate that the Blaster worm might have been created by a gang of Chinese computer hackers called Xfocus. It isn't known who Xfocus is or what their agenda is, nor is it known if Xfocus has any connections to the Chinese government, and it isn't clear if Xfocus created the Welchia or Sasser worms.

Parson's current whereabouts and activities are not known. He is presumably out of prison, but it isn't known if he has resumed his hacking or not.

Bibliography

Associated Press. "FBI Arrests Teen in 'Blaster' Attack." 29 August 2003. foxnews.com. Wire Service News Article. 27 May 2013.

NBC News Today Show. "'I'm not the one they need to get'." 2 September 2003. nbcnews.com. Transcript of 'Today' show exclusive interview with worm suspect. 27 May 2013.

US District Court Western District of Washington at Seattle. "Plea Agreement in U.S. Jeffrey Lee Parson." 27 March 2005. rbs2.com. Court Documents. 27 May 2013.

Wikipedia. "Blaster (computer worm)." n.d. en.wikipedia.org. Online Encyclopedia Entry. 27 May 2013.

The Man behind the Great Cyber Heist: Albert Gonzalez

No criminal has done more to demonstrate the power of the internet for larceny than Albert Gonzalez. The Miami hacker figured out how to steal from 180 million victims at once through one of the biggest identity thefts in history. He did it while working as an informant for the U.S. Secret Service, who was supposed to be helping the feds catch other cyber crooks.

A Life of Cyber Crime

Albert Gonzalez's life story reads like a history of cybercrime over the years – he went from high school hacker to hardened criminal. Like many hackers, Gonzalez started out stealing information, but eventually figured out how to commit cyber theft on a massive scale.

Gonzalez grew up in Miami, and his father, Alberto Gonzalez Sr., was a first generation American, a refugee from Castro's Cuba who worked as a landscaper. Gonzalez bought his first computer when he was 12 and got interested in hacking and security when his computer got infected by a virus he had downloaded.

Within a few years, Gonzalez had graduated to black hat hacking (or stealing information). He hacked a NASA computer when he was just 14 and had the experience of being visited at his high school by the FBI. The incident made Gonzalez famous. He organized his own gang of hackers and gave an interview to ZDNET under the name "Soupnazi" after the popular character from *Seinfeld.* In the interview, Gonzalez bragged about defacing websites.

Hacking for Fun and Profit

Even though Gonzalez tried to portray himself as a fun-loving hacker out to "stick it to the man," he was already an experienced identity thief. When he wasn't vandalizing sites, Gonzalez was stealing credit card numbers and using them to order CDs and other items. He had the items delivered to empty houses in his neighborhood to cover his tracks. Since he was too young to drive, Gonzalez had a friend drive him over to pick up the loot during lunch period at his high school.

Albert Gonzalez was definitely a genius – he taught himself how to hack internet service providers (ISPs) by reading technical manuals. He was one of the first to figure out how to hack Wi-Fi and one of the first Wardrivers (hackers that log on through wireless networks).

After dropping out of college, Gonzalez stumbled onto a treasure trove of data for a hacker: computers belonging to executives such as IT managers. The computers contained such valuable information as network diagrams and system architecture.

Working for and Against the Secret Service

By 2003, Albert Gonzalez had left Miami for the New York City area, and once there he worked as a security consultant at an internet company in New Jersey. That was only one of many activities Gonzalez engaged in – he also liked to cash out. Gonzalez would steal debit card numbers and make his own debit cards and PIN numbers, then go to ATM machines and use them to clean out all the cash in an account.

A New York police detective caught Gonzalez cashing out a Manhattan ATM in July 2003. That led to his first arrest and the attention of the Secret Service. The Service and the U.S. Attorney were looking for an informant that would help them infiltrate Shadowcrew.com, a network of hundreds of cyber criminals all over the world.

In exchange for not being prosecuted, Gonzalez was able to identify a dozen members of the Shadowcrew to the Secret Service. Gonzalez was so helpful to the agency and a federal anti-hacking program called Operation Firewall that he was even asked to speak to conferences of federal agents. Operation Firewall involved a sort of discussion board for hackers where Gonzalez served as administrator. The hackers didn't realize that federal agents were monitoring their chat until they were arrested.

What the Secret Service didn't realize was that Gonzalez was still an active criminal who was organizing a massive identity theft ring. He wasn't planning to steal hundreds of credit card numbers, he was planning to steal millions and he almost got away with it.

Get Rich or Die Trying

Even as he was turning in some hackers, Gonzalez was recruiting his own elite gang of hackers for one of the biggest cyber thefts in history. Gonzalez reportedly recruited some big-name hackers to help him, including Jonathan James, Stephen Watt, and Christopher Scott.

Gonzalez also recruited a number of confederates overseas, including the Ukrainian mastermind known as Maksym Yastremski, who was known as the internet's top fence for stolen credit and debit card information. From 2004-2006, he reportedly made $11 million selling the stolen cards. Other hackers were recruited in Belarus, the Ukraine, Estonia, and China.

The gang called themselves "Operation Get Rich or Die Trying." Gonzalez certainly did his best to achieve the get rich part. He stayed at expensive hotels and once reportedly spent $75,000 on a birthday party.

Stealing from 250,000 Businesses at Once

The way Operation Get Rich or Die Trying worked was simple – the crooks placed malware in the networks of large corporations. The targets included Heartland Payment Systems, which processed credit card payments for 250,000 businesses and some of the biggest names in American retail. Boston Market, OfficeMax, TJ Maxx, Dave & Buster's, Barnes & Noble, Target, and DSW were among the targets.

The malware they used consisted of sniffer worms designed to detect and capture credit card numbers. The sniffers were created by Stephen Watt, a legendary hacker from the 1990s who had a reputation as a good guy.

The sniffers were placed by members of the ring who would drive up and down highways on the East Coast. They would use wardriving equipment to scan various businesses until they found a network that they could place a sniffer in, and when they could place a sniffer, the haul was usually massive. They stole 5,000 card numbers from a Dave & Buster's restaurant in Islandia, N.Y. alone and used the numbers to steal $600,000.

Let's Go Shopping

The gang also succeeded into getting into the network at the headquarters of TJX through one of its subsidiaries, Marshalls. At TJX, they hacked the server that contained old credit transaction data and installed a sniffer that would seek out and capture the most recent transaction data, then send it to Gonzalez's computer in Miami.

Another method Gonzalez and his gang pioneered was to simply steal cash registers from stores like OfficeMax. They took the registers apart and cracked the computers inside to learn how they worked. They also hacked Micros Systems, which manufactured cash registers in order to locate passwords for point of sale systems that accepted credit card transactions at stores.

Federal agents learned that a massive identity theft ring was at work when TJX executives contacted them in 2006. The owner of the department stores TJ Maxx and Marshalls had discovered that hackers had been stealing card numbers from its database for over a year. In 2007 the Secret Service got a similar complaint from Dave & Busters. Even though the Service knew that a massive identity theft ring was at work, they didn't know who was behind it, nor did they realize that their star informant was the mastermind.

Capturing the Mastermind

The Secret Service finally tracked Gonzalez down through Maskym Yastremski, the credit card fence. Agents managed to hack the fence's laptop and learn he was buying large numbers of card numbers from a mysterious provider in America, yet they learned he didn't know who the provider was.

When the Ukrainian was arrested in Turkey in July 2007, police learned he had been asked to procure a fake passport for one of the American provider's henchmen. The henchman needed to get out of the U.S. because he had been arrested with $200,000 in cash and 80 blank debit cards. The cash came from ATM machines. By checking with cops around the U.S., the Secret Service identified the henchman as Jonathan Williams. When agents checked Williams' possessions, they found a thumb drive that contained the address of Gonzalez's sister, yet they still had no direct connection to Gonzalez.

That changed when an agent turned up an email address belonging to the criminal mastermind that Yastremski was trading instant messages with. The address was soupnazi@efnet.ru. The Secret Service recognized it as Gonzalez's address and moved against him and his gang in Miami. Agents knew he had been using the name Soupnazi for many years. Now that they knew who they were after, agents knew exactly where to find Albert Gonzalez in Miami.

End of the Line

Gonzalez was arrested in an expensive suite at the National Hotel in Miami Beach in May 2008. Gonzalez started cooperating with authorities and even led authorities to a barrel buried in his parents' backyard that contained $1.2 million in cash. In 2009, he pleaded guilty to 19 charges of hacking. In March 25, 2010, Gonzalez was sentenced to 20 years in prison. He later tried to withdraw his plea bargain.

Gonzalez is currently serving his sentence at a federal prison in Michigan. If he behaves himself, he'll be released in 2025. It isn't known how much cash he has stashed on the outside, but it's doubtful that Albert Gonzalez will be a poor man when he walks out of prison.

Bibliography

Guarino, Mark. "Card hacker Albert Gonzalez gets 20 years but cyber-crime rising." 26 March 2010. csmonitor.com. Christian Science Monitor Article. 29 May 2013.

Lush, Tamara. "Fla. man in credit card data theft accepts plea deal." 28 August 2009. csmonitor.com. Associated Press Wire Service News Article. 29 May 2013.

Poulsen, Kevin. "Feds Charge 11 in Breaches at TJ Maxx, OfficeMax, DSW, Others." 5 August 2008. wired.com. Wired News Article. 29 May 2013.

Suddath, Claire. "Master Hacker Albert Gonzalez." 19 August 2009. time.com. Time Magazine Feature. 29 May 2013.

Verini, James. "The Great Cyberheist." 10 November 2010. nytimes.com. New York Times Magazine Feature Article. 29 May 2013.

Wikipedia. "Albert Gonzalez." n.d. en.wikipedia.org. Online Encyclopedia Entry. 29 May 2013.

The Zombie Master:
Jeanson James Ancheta

If there is a most hated hacker in the world, it has to be Jeanson James Ancheta, the evil genius known as the Zombie Master. The high school dropout figured out a means of using botnets, secret networks of computers that unleash thousands of pieces of spam email, to attack hundreds and thousands of computers at once. Ancheta also figured out how to help some of the most obnoxious criminals online cover their tracks and target thousands of victims at once.

If you want somebody to blame for all the spam that keeps clogging your inbox and Facebook page, blame Jeanson James Ancheta. The zombie master, or botmaster, made the internet safe for spammers and unsafe for everybody else. If there is a cyber-hell, Ancheta deserves a special place in it for the avalanche of garbage he unleashed upon innocent computer users all over the world.

From Drop Out to Master Cyber Criminal

In 2004, Jeanson James Ancheta was something of a harmless loser, a nerd who hung around the old neighborhood in Downey, Calif. near South Central Los Angeles. He was a high school dropout who had attended a program for learning disabled students. To people who saw him, Ancheta looked like just another twenty-something failure who worked at an internet café. Yet he was a major league cybercriminal.

Ancheta's career as a criminal mastermind for hire began when he discovered a computer program called rxbot, which created large numbers of bots, or software robots, software applications that perform automated tasks online. Ancheta figured out how to use it to create botnets, or swarms of bots, for malicious purposes.

An example of such a bot would be an
application that sends out spam. Ancheta could
create one that would come onto a computer via
a tapeworm or Trojan virus, then start sending
out spam from that computer. The computer of a
person that clicked on one of Ancheta's pieces
of spam would then start sending out more
spam.

Rent a Zombie

The bots Ancheta created were called zombies,
because they are mindless creatures that
perform the same task over and over again, just
like the stock horror movie monsters. He quickly
became part of an online underworld that rented
zombies out to other criminals.

A hacker might rent a zombie in order to send out a Trojan virus to steal information. An identity thief might rent a zombie to send spam in a phishing scam to steal personal information, such as bank account numbers or Social Security numbers from unsuspecting users.

Ancheta turned zombies into big business; he is believed to have infected as many as 400,000 PCs with viruses. Ancheta turned the infected PCs into a massive bot net that could send out millions of pieces of spam. He then rented them out to customers that included organized crime, con artists, spies, identify thieves, and other cyber predators.

Excellent Customer Service

The U.S. Justice Department even alleged that Ancheta advertised his services through the Botnet Underground. He apparently had hundreds of customers and made thousands of dollars with his botnet. The botnets reported back to Ancheta through an Internet Relay Chat channel.

They were built using the rxbot Trojan horse program and sent out to perform their task. Ancheta gave excellent service to his customers; he even wrote an instruction manual for them. Each botnet was custom created to perform a specific task, such as sending out adware.

Each botnet was rented out for around $3,000. Ancheta was well aware of the fact that his customers were spamming and carrying out denial of service attacks. He made a total of between $58,000 and $60,000 in just three months from his activities.

The Botnet Comes Crashing Down

Like many criminals, Ancheta was probably defeated by his own ego and greed. He apparently got too ambitious when he went after one of America's most secret and secure military installations, the Weapons Division of the U.S. Naval Air Warfare Center in China Lake, Calif.

In December 2004, FBI agents who were cracking down on the Botmaster Underground showed up at Ancheta's home with a warrant. Federal cyber-sleuths had been able to track the Zombie Master to his lair. Once there, they confiscated two computers that contained rxbot and were used to control the botnet army. The FBI then called Ancheta to the local field office so he could pick up the computers; Ancheta made the mistake of coming in and found himself under arrest.

Ancheta was charged with 17 different federal crimes, including conspiracy, attempted transmission of code to a protected computer, transmission of code to a government computer, and accessing a protected computer to commit fraud and money laundering.

Ancheta plead guilty in federal court in Los Angeles in January 2006. He was ordered to forfeit the $58,000 he had made and sell his 1993 BMW. Ancheta was also ordered to pay $15,000 restitution to the federal government for infecting the military computers. In May 2006, the Zombie Master was sentenced to five years in prison for his activities.

Ancheta has presumably served his sentence by now. His present activities and locations are unknown, so it is not certain if he is still an active hacker or not. News reports indicate that Ancheta had unknown associates at the time of his arrest. It isn't known if those associates were arrested, but the Botnet Underground is very much alive, even if Ancheta is no longer part of it.

Bibliography

Spam Daily News. "Alleged zombie master
arrested." 3 November 2005.
spamdailnews.com. News Blog Entry. 27 May
2013.

—. "Organized crime offers renta-a-zombie
deals." 25 May 2005. spamdailynews.com. News
Blog Entry. 27 May 2013.

—. "Zombie master Jeanson Ancheta pleads
guilty." 23 January 2006. spamdialynews.com.
News Blog Entry. 27 May 2013.

—. "Zombie Master Jeanson Ancheta sentenced
to 5 years in prison." 9 May 2006.
spamdailynews.com. News Blog Entry. 27 May
2013.

US Department of Justice. "Bot-Herder Jeanson James Ancheta Jailed." 23 January 2006. secure64.com. US Justice Department Press Release. 27 May 2013.

Vamosi, Robert. "Cybercrime does pay: here's how." 27 January 2006. reviews.cent.com. CNET Feature Article. 27 May 2013.

Wikipedia. "Internet Bot." n.d. en.wikipedia.org. Online Encyclopedia Entry. 27 May 2013.

The Big Wardriver: Adam Botbyl

There are some hackers that don't even need a direct Internet connection to get online; they're called Wardrivers. Wardrivers cruise around in a moving vehicle looking for networks to hack into so they can get online for free.

Another reason why wardrivers do this is so they can cover their tracks and use somebody else's Wi-Fi for their illegal activities. That makes it harder but not impossible for cyber sleuths to track them down. One of the most notorious Wardrivers is Adam Botbyl, a Michigan resident who allegedly stole $2.5 million from the Lowe's home improvement store chain using the technique.

Wardriving itself is one of those grey areas in cyberspace. Theoretically, it is legal to wardrive because all you're doing is receiving a radio signal. Yet it is illegal to enter somebody else's network without permission. It is also illegal to use somebody else's network for your purposes.

Wardriving for Fun and Profit

Adam Botbyl achieved infamy in 2003 when he and another hacker named Paul Timmins went out for a drive in Michigan in 2003. One of the networks the two came upon was at a Lowe's home improvement store.

Botbyl allegedly used Lowe's network to access his email, which was a crime at the time. Lowe's, fearing that hackers were trying to steal information, called in the FBI, which tracked the two down. Timmins was charged with hacking and became one of the first people charged with a wardriving-related crime. He later pleaded guilty and went to federal prison.

Botbyl realized that Lowe's wireless network, which connected stores around the United States and Canada with the company's headquarters in North Carolina, had a serious security hole. He could get in and steal information, including credit card data.

Stealing from Lowe's

Despite Timmins' arrest, Botbyl decided to become a big-time criminal with the help of a convicted hacker named Brian Salcedo. Salcedo was on probation for another computer-related crime.

The two hacked into Lowe's wireless network on October 25, 2003; they first got into the company's headquarters network then into stores around the United States. They thought that they hit the jackpot when they discovered Tcpcredit, an application that processed credit card purchases. The two decided to do a little shopping on the night of November 5, 2003.

On that night they set up shop in the parking lot of the Lowe's store in Southfield, Michigan. There they were able to get into the computers of a store that was still open in Long Beach, Calif., and tried to capture credit card transactions. Instead of capturing transactions, it caused a number of computerized cash registers at the Lowe's in Long Beach to crash.

The FBI Throws a Net over the Wardrivers

Lowe's IT department realized that somebody was trying to hack its network and contacted the FBI. The FBI's Cyber Crime Division looked into the matter and managed to track the hacking back to Southfield.

Salcedo and Botbyl returned to the Lowe's parking lot on November 7, 2003, and inserted their own version of Tcpcredit into Lowe's network. This version would capture copies of Lowe's customers' credit card information and transmit it back to the cyber predators.

The wireless bandits didn't realize that the FBI was watching them. FBI agents were watching the parking lot and spotted their 1991 Buick Grand Prix with antennas on it. When the FBI checked with Lowe's, they found that Botbyl's version of Tcpcredit had already been loaded at two Lowe's stores. Fortunately for Lowe's customers, the FBI shut the fake version down after just six credit card numbers had been stolen.

When Botbyl and Salcedo returned on November 10, 2003, they were arrested by FBI agents, and their wardriving equipment was confiscated. Their shopping spree had ended before it began.

Wardrivers in Prison

Adam Botbyl ended up facing 16 charges in federal court, including conspiracy, computer fraud, wire fraud, unauthorized computer access, intentional transmission of computer code, and attempted possession of unauthorized access devices. The last charges refer to stolen passwords. His attempt at wardriving fraud ended before it began.

Botbyl eventually pleaded guilty, served 26 months in a federal prison, and received two years' supervised release. Brian Salcedo wasn't so lucky; he received nine years in prison, probably because he was on probation at the time of his caper. The release ended on January 28, 2008. Botbyl's current activities are hard to determine; he maintains a blog, where he discusses hacking and computer security. He also maintains a presence on LinkedIn. It looks like Botbyl has quit wardriving and seems to be working as a computer consultant.

Among other things, he now gives advice on how to steal songs from iTunes and how to use free software applications like Ubuntu. He also gives tips and code that are supposed to enable users to hack Apple's operating system, OS X Lion. One has to wonder how long it will be before Adam Botbyl ends up back behind bars.

Bibliography

Botbyl, Adam. "Notes from the desk of Adam Botbyl." n.d. adambotbyl.com. Blog. 27 May 2013.

Poulsen, Kevin. "Michigan Wi-Fi Hacker jailed for nine years." 16 December 2004. theregister.co.uk. News Article. 27 May 2013.

Vamosi, Robert. "Real-world war driving arrests." 17 September 2004. reviews.cnet.com. CNET Feature Article. 27 May 2013.

Wikipedia. "Adam Botbyl." n.d. en.wikipedia.org. Online Encyclopedia Entry. 27 May 2013.

Wikipeida. "Wardriving." n.d. en.wikpedia.org. ONline Encyclopedia Entry. 27 May 2013.

The Man Called the Analyzer: Ehud Tenenbaum

Legendary computer hackers get nicknames just like other famous criminals. Such a legend is Ehud "the Analyzer" Tenenbaum, the man who hacked the Pentagon when he was just 18-years old. Fourteen years later Tenenbaum made headlines again by masterminding a bank job that netted $10 million.

Tenenbaum is typical of a lot of hackers who start out as arrogant teenaged nerds out to prove what they can do. Like many hackers, Tenenbaum's focus has changed from simply hacking to prove his skills to enriching his bank account.

Like some other hackers, Tenenbaum may have friends in high places, or rather intelligence agencies, that are protecting him. In particular, he might be Israeli's secret weapon in its cyber wars against its enemies. Even though he is a criminal, the Analyzer also seems to be a patriot who is always willing to battle his country's enemies.

Let's Hack the Pentagon

The Analyzer is a legend who has worked for and against his nation and its allies. He was born Ramat HaSharon but goes by the name Ehud Tenenbaum. Tenenbaum is a native of Israel, who operates out of that country but has cohorts all over the world.

The Analyzer first attracted attention in 1998 when he was able to hack computers at the Pentagon, U.S. Air Force Headquarters, the U.S. Navy, NASA, and Lawrence Livermore National Laboratory, where America's nuclear weapons are designed. He also targeted MIT and other U.S. universities. Closer to home, Tenenbaum hacked computers for the Israeli Defense Forces; Israel's parliament, the Knesset; and the office of Israel's president.

His attacks were so effective and blatant that a special task force of agents from the FBI, the Air Force, NASA, the CIA, the National Security Agency, and Defense Information Systems Agency was set up to capture him. News reports indicate that the U.S. government was so worried that President Bill Clinton was briefed about the effort to catch him.

The Most Effective Attack on the Pentagon

Ehud Tenenbaum became a celebrity at age 18 when he was revealed as the genius who had hacked into 700 websites worldwide. Tenenbaum was offered movie deals and jobs. Israel's Prime Minister, Benjamin Netanyahu, called Tenenbaum "damn good" and "dangerous too."

Many Israelis were proud of Tenenbaum and his abilities even though his activities were highly illegal. The Pentagon may have been worried about Tenenbaum, but the Israeli government may have made use of him.

Interestingly enough, the U.S. military was afraid that Saddam Hussein's government was behind the attack. It was later proven that Tenenbaum was working with two California teenagers named Mac and Stimpy. It isn't known if they were simply shills or part of the attack.

Tenenbaum pleaded not guilty to the Pentagon attack and served eight months in prison. He also served briefly in the Israeli Defense Forces but may have been released to serve his country in other ways.

Secret Cyber Warrior for Israel

Over the years Tenenbaum has admitted to targeting some of Israel's enemies, including the radical Palestinian terrorist organizations. He also destroyed the website of the radical Shiite organization Hamas. There have also been massive cyber attacks on peace groups and dissidents in Israel. Some leftists have accused Tenenbaum of being responsible for those attacks; Tenenbaum's company 2XS and a shadowy group called the Israeli Internet Underground.

It isn't known whether Tenenbaum had anything to do with the Stuxnet worm that attacked and disabled Iran's nuclear facilities in 2010. The worm is known to have originated in Israel and the head of the Israeli Defense Forces claimed credit for it. Stuxnet was capable of destroying Iranian nuclear weapons manufacturing equipment. Tenenbaum served in the Defense Forces. There is a strong possibility that the Analyzer was involved in its creation. One of Tenenbaum's specialties is creating worms.

Involvement with Stuxnet might explain why Tenenbaum has been able to get off so easily for some of his other activities. He was able to escape serious prison time for the Pentagon hacking and for multimillion-dollar bank robberies.

Getting Away with the $10 Million Bank Job

In 2008 Canadian authorities arrested Ehud Tenenbaum as the main suspect in a scheme to steal $1.5 million from banks in Canada. Interestingly enough, U.S. authorities filed an extradition request for Tenenbaum, which was quickly honored. He was taken to the U.S. and held in U.S. custody even though he was an Israeli citizen and he had committed his crimes in Canada.

A strong possibility is that U.S. intelligence agencies interceded with the Canadian government to get Tenenbaum released. He was allowed to get away even though the scheme he was involved with may have resulted in $10 million in losses to various banks all over the world. Authorities might consider him too important an asset to go to prison.

It is also interesting to note that Tenenbaum received a sentence of three years' probation and a $503,000 fine for his role in a $10 million theft. It sounds as if intelligence agencies were able to intercede with prosecutors in order to win the Analyzer's release.

Israel's Secret Cyber Weapon

The Analyzer's current activities and whereabouts are unknown. It is a strong possibility that U.S. and Israeli intelligence agencies know exactly where he is because he is working well at what he is doing. Israel has probably put the Analyzer to work to take out its enemies. The Analyzer was released just as President Obama was stepping up cyber-attacks against Iran.

The Analyzer might just be Israel's secret weapon in cyber warfare. The hacker is fighting for his country while lining his bank account.

Bibliography

LasRosa, Mary. "The Comskybot Code: Conduct in the Time of Terror." 1 November 2003. dissidentvoice.org. Blog Entry. 26 May 2013.

Sanger, David E. "Obama Order Sped Up Wave of Cyber attacks Against Iran." 1 June 2012. en.wikipedia.org. New York Times Investigative News Article. 26 May 2013.

Sinai, Liron. "Canada: Israel hacker suspected of involvement in major fraud case." 5 September 2008. ynetnews.com. Israeli Wire Service News Article. 26 May 2013.

Trounson, Rebecca. "Hacker Case Taps into Fame, Fury." 27 April 1998. articles.latimes.com. Los Angeles Times News Article. 26 May 2013.

Wikipedia. "Ehud Tenenbaum." n.d. en.wikipedia.org. Online Encyclopedia Entry. 26 May 2013.

—. "Stuxnet." n.d. en.wikipedia.org. Online Encyclopedia Entry. 26 May 2013.

Ynet. "US: Plea bargain for "The Analyzer"." 8 July 2012. ynetnews.com. Israeli Wire Service news Article. 26 May 2013.

The Mindphaser: Chad Davis and Global Hell

Chad Davis, or the Mindphaser, achieved fame or rather infamy at age 19 by declaring war on the United States government. Incensed that FBI agents had searched his home, Davis started hacking high-profile targets, including the webpages for the FBI itself, the U.S. Army, and the White House.

Davis and his merry band of hackers, which called itself Global Hell, found themselves in a cyber-war with the FBI in early 1999. The battle between the hackers and the federal cyber sleuths became a preview of many such battles in the years ahead. Authorities tried to clamp down on hackers while hackers ramped up their attacks in an attempt to demonstrate their power.

Chad Davis might not have been the best or the most effective hacker, but he was certainly one of the bravest. At one point he even managed to shut down the FBI's website with a denial of service attack. As a reward, Davis became one of the first hackers to feel the full weight of the power of the U.S. Department of Justice; he wouldn't be the last.

The Mindphaser from Green Bay

Not too much is known about Chad Davis's background or personal life. He was from Green Bay, Wis., and he was born in 1981, according to media accounts. By 1999, when he was 19, Davis was deeply involved in something called globalHell, or Global Hell.

Global Hell was a pioneering syndicate of computer hackers whose members included Patrick W. Gregory, who went by the screen name of MostHateD. News reports indicate that Chad Davis was one of the founders of Global Hell. The organizations goals or purpose are not known, but its activities became very famous.

Like some hackers, Davis seemed to believe that he had a right to hack, and he resented any attempt by authorities to interfere with that "right." Ironically enough, it was federal attempts to intimidate him that led Davis to commit his famous exploits.

Global Hell Strikes Back

The FBI first searched Davis's home in Green Bay on June 2, 1999, as part of a crackdown on globalHell. The agents didn't arrest Davis, but they let him know that they were watching him. During the raid, agents found a beer in his refrigerator and fined him $168 because he was too young to drink.

Davis got his revenge on June 28, 1999, when he hacked the U.S. Army's website and posted the words: "Global Hell is alive. Global hell will not die." Over the next few weeks Global Hell operatives defaced the websites for the White House and the FBI as well as the Army. They also struck out at several large corporations.

The raid on Davis's home had been prompted by a May 9 incident in which swear words were smeared all over the White House website. The group also knocked out the FBI site with a denial of service attack on May 26, 1999. It isn't known whether Davis was involved in these attacks or not.

Uncle Sam Strikes Back

The FBI struck back with an all-out offensive against Global Hell that involved the questioning of its members. Like other criminals, the hackers proved willing to rat out their colleagues when faced with law enforcement pressure. At least two of the group's members told the FBI they were looking for Mindphaser.

The federal sleuths were able to link Mindphaser to Davis and to start monitoring his home. On the night of June 27–28, 1999, when Davis hacked the U.S. Army website, FBI agents were monitoring his computer and telephone. They knew that the attack on the Army website was launched from Davis's telephone line.

Davis was arrested shortly after the attack on the Army. On Jan. 4, 2000, Davis pleaded guilty to the hacking and was sentenced to six months in prison. Davis also had to pay $8,054 in restitution even though he had reportedly caused over $1 million in damage to government systems.

A Pioneer Cyber Warrior

In a way, Chad Davis was a sort of pioneer; by showing how vulnerable government websites were to attack, he demonstrated the power and possibilities of cyber warfare. Davis paved the way for government sponsored cyber warriors like those in China and Israel.

Global Hell's tactics were later adopted by politically motivated "Hacktivist" groups such as Anonymous. These groups have a specific agenda and use hacking to achieve it. Anonymous is motivated by anarchist ideals and hatred of big government and big business similar to the ideas that motivated Global Hell.

Davis and Global Hell were pioneers in another way; they went legit. Like a number of top hackers, Global Hell decided to start marketing its services to the enemy, namely big business, as cyber security experts. Global Hell even put out a press release in September 1999 that announced it was going legit and selling its services.

Off the Grid or Is He?

Like many hackers, Chad Davis has dropped off the grid since his days of fame. His current whereabouts and activities are unknown, although online rumors indicate that he is now a "security consultant" for large corporations. That means he is still active but on the other side. One strong possibility is that Chad Davis is now working for the government he once targeted and using his skills on behalf of the FBI and other agencies.

Bibliography

Burke, Lynn. "MostHateD to Plead Most Guilty."
29 March 2000. wired.com. Wired News Article.
28 May 2013.

Meeks, Brock. "Global Hell says it's going legit."
7 September 1999. zdnet.com. Zdnet News
Article. 28 May 2013.

Suro, Robert. "The Hackers Who Won't Quit." 1
September 1999. washingtonpost.com.
Washington Post Feature Article. 28 May 2013.

U.S. Department of Justice. "Chad Davis,
"Global Hell" Hacker, Sentenced to Six Months
in Prison, Three Years' Probation For Air Force
Network Hacks." 1 March 2000. 4law.co.li.
Justice Department Press Release. 28 May
2013.

Wikipedia. "Chad Davis." n.d. en.wikipedia.com. Online Encyclopedia Entry. 28 May 2013.

The Saint of the Internet: Raphael Gray

Not every hacker is a bad guy or a criminal; some hackers are just honorable people trying to expose flaws in security. That was definitely the case of Raphael Gray, or the Saint; he simply went out to show average people that their credit card data was vulnerable to cyber predators and found an FBI agent knocking on his door.

That was extraordinary enough because Gray lived in a remote village in Wales in the United Kingdom. The extraordinary response to Gray's activities was prompted by the incredible acts he had committed; the 19-year-old hacker had 23,000 credit card numbers from an online database.

Gray also demonstrated his abilities by stealing the credit card information of Microsoft founder Bill Gates, then the world's richest man. He used Gates' credit card number to order Viagra (a treatment for male sexual dysfunction) from an online drugstore and sent it to Gates' office at Microsoft headquarters in Redmond, Washington. The Saint's motive for this crime was a noble one: to try and alert Microsoft and Gates to huge holes in their security.

The Do Gooder Who Was Ignored

Gray's cybercrimes were not motivated by greed or arrogance but by a desire to do the right thing. The young man, who went by the screen names of "The Saint" and "Curador," wanted to protect people from cyber predators. Yet he found himself under arrest and even facing psychiatric attention from the British National Health Service.

Gray's odyssey began in 1999, when he hacked into several top e-commerce sites in January and February 1999 from his home computer. Gray was shocked by how easy it was to crack the sites and steal credit card data. He tried to alert authorities and executives at e-commerce companies. Nobody seemed to listen to or care what he was saying.

Gray tried other means; he set up a hall of shame that showed the cracks in security and e-commerce sites. He even posted 6,500 stolen credit card numbers online in an attempt to show what was wrong.

From Internet Porn to the Saint

Raphael Gray said he was introduced to the Internet when a friend showed him how to find porn over it when he was around 13 years old. Gray also said he started writing computer programs when he was just 11 years old.

He was soon fooling around and eventually graduated to hacking. Like many hackers of his generation, he was inspired to try and crack military sites by the silly movie *WarGames*.

Gray stumbled upon the flaws in e-commerce security in 1999 while shopping online. At the time, online shopping was popular due to the e-commerce revolution. He soon found programs that would download credit card numbers to his PC. The Saint also created a program that hunted out vulnerable sites and stole more credit card numbers.

Eventually Gray discovered an online black market for credit card numbers. A cyber crook in the United States even offered him $15 for each of his stolen credit card numbers. Instead of getting overtaken by greed, Gray got incensed and decided to do something.

"Law enforcement couldn't hack its way out of a wet paper bag."

The Saint's crusade for security expanded and started attracting attention. Gray was interviewed by a news website, and he made some comments to radio. Those comments were heard by another hacker, a security consultant named Chris Davis. Davis, incensed by Gray's arrogance, located the Saint's ISP and contacted the Royal Canadian Mounted Police. The Mounties contacted the FBI and Scotland Yard and gave them Gray's address.

The comments Gray made to the media included: "Law Enforcement couldn't hack its way out of a wet paper bag." He was obviously wrong because in March 2000, four uniformed Welsh constables, an FBI agent, and two inspectors from Scotland Yard came knocking on the door of Gray's family cottage.

Interestingly enough, Gray said the constables who came to his home didn't even know what some of his equipment was. He was arrested and charged with violating the Computer Misuse Act. The charges included "using a computer to gain unauthorized access to a system to break the law"; in other words, hacking.

Mentally Ill or a Hero

Even though he may have done $3.5 million worth of damage, a court sentenced Gray to three years of probation. Since he had been diagnosed with schizophrenia, Gray was ordered to see a psychiatrist every week. Gray told the BBC that he had received three job offers after his case was publicized.

It isn't known what Raphael Gray is doing today or where he's living. Like many hackers, he's dropped off the grid, although he's probably working in cyber security somewhere. Most likely the Saint now tests online security for a living by working as a "security consultant."

A bigger question remains: Did the Saint do the world a service by exposing the holes in online security or not? He obviously forced retailers to beef up their security, but through his actions, Gray also showed other criminals how easy it would be to steal online. Thirteen years after Gray's brush with fame, cyber security still remains a concern, and public distrust of e-commerce websites remains high. The Saint, like many other "saints," was ultimately punished for his good deeds and possibly for his sins.

Bibliography

Andrews, Robert. "Sins of the 'saint of e-commerce'." 6 July 2001. news.bbc.co.uk. BBC News Story. 29 May 2013.

BBC News. "Teen hacker escapes jail sentence." 6 July 2001. news.bbc.co.uk. BBC News Story. 29 May 2013.

—. "Teenage hacker admits website charges." 28 March 2001. news.bbc.uk. BBC News Story. 29 May 2013.

—. "The hacker who sent Viagra to Bill Gates." 1 July 2001. news.bbc.co.uk. BBC Feature Story. 29 May 2013.

Corbin, Jane. "Teenage hackers target security flaws." 3 July 2000. news.bbc.co.uk. BBC Panorama Feature Story. 29 May 2013.

Leyden, John. "'Bill Gates' hacker escapes jail." 6 July 2001. theregister.co.uk. Register News Story. 29 May 2013.

Los Angeles Times. "Bill Gates Among Victims of Hackers." 26 March 2000. articles.latimes.com. Los Angeles Times News Brief. 29 May 2013.

PBS Frontline. "interview: Raphael gray a.k.a. curador." n.d. pbs.org. Interview Transcript. 29 May 2013.

Reed, Robyn. "Raphael Gray internet "hacker" exposes Microsoft Security weaknesses ." 21 March 2001. mjreedsolicitors.co.uk. Blog Post. 29 May 2013.

Wikipedia. "Raphael Gray." n.d. en.wikipedia.org. Online Encyclopedia Entry. 29 May 2013.

A Hacker for Good: Samy Kamkar

Samy Kamkar might just be the ultimate white hat hacker fighting for the rights of the average person while embarrassing some of the world's biggest corporations. Kamkar's creations have caused just as much commotion in the real world as in cyberspace. His findings led to congressional hearings and class action suits.

Kamkar is the one who exposed the tracking of wireless device users by Apple, Google, and Microsoft. He's also the person who exposed the weaknesses in MySpace and later in some of the world's largest electronic payment systems, including Visa and MasterCard.

Kamkar's story also reveals the absurdities of the hacker lifestyle. His security company was actually raided by the United States Secret Service, and he was prosecuted under the USA Patriot Act. Kamkar has also earned the hatred of a lot of black hat or criminal hackers by showing the public the tricks of their trade.

Samy Is My Hero

Samy Kamkar first achieved attention in 2005 by releasing the Samy Worm, or Samy (XSS). This was the first self-propagating worm detected; that meant the worm could actually make copies of itself. Some experts believe the Samy Worm was the fastest spreading computer virus of all time.

Kamkar demonstrated the worm's capabilities by releasing it on MySpace, the first popular social networking site. The worm caused computers to crash and left users with the words "but most of all Samy is my hero" on their screens. Within 20 hours of the Samy Worm's release, MySpace had crashed and over one million computers had been infected.

Samy had demonstrated the power and potential of computer worms. He also earned the enmity of Uncle Sam. In 2006 federal agents raided his office and arrested him for releasing the virus. His punishment was one of the worst ones a hacker could face; he was prohibited from using a computer for three years.

The Crusading Hacker

After his ban from computer use was lifted in 2009, Kamkar established himself as a crusading hacker. He began exposing the problems with the Internet and abuses of power by large corporations. His first exposé was of smart credit and debit cards that used wireless technology to communicate with computer networks. Kamkar showed how easy it was to hack such cards and steal financial data.

Samy also started traveling and speaking at numerous conferences. He even helped activists in the European nation of Slovakia expose corruption in their government.

Then there was Evercookie, a cookie that could not be deleted. The purpose of this cookie was to spur discussion and give designers better tools for the prevention of future cookies. Kamkar was moved to action by media reports that large companies like Fox and Universal were using cookies to track users' online activities for advertising purposes.

Taking on Google, Apple, and Microsoft

Kamkar's next targets included tech icons such as Google and Steve Jobs of Apple. In 2011 Kamkar discovered that Google was tracking users of its wireless network. He showed reporters how a person could track down a user's physical location through its Wi-Fi network. His work was even detailed in front-page stories in *The Wall Street Journal* and *The New York Times*.

Kamkar also made the interesting discovery that Google was maintaining a huge secret database that collated its users' movements. That meant Google could pinpoint the physical location of those logging on to its Android wireless operating system. He also discovered that Apple and Microsoft had similar capabilities.

Samy even mapped out phone users' homes by using information he collected from the databases. This was done by discovering the location of the Wi-Fi router a person was using. If that wasn't bad enough, he learned that GPS coordinates of users were being transmitted back to Google.

In a demonstration for the BBC, Kamkar showed that Internet users could find a person's physical address through Firefox and other web browsers. He even created a website that did this automatically.

Kamkar's revelation spurred congressional action; the House of Representatives held hearings and questioned representatives of the tech giants. Many people were worried that stalkers could use the technology to locate individuals.

The Lone Ranger of the Internet

Samy Kamkar is a sort of Lone Ranger of the Internet. Even though his exploits are well known, little is known about his personal life or background. Like the Lone Ranger, he fights for justice with various good deeds yet never reveals anything about himself.

That's a very strange side to a man who once told a journalist: "Privacy is dead, people, I'm sorry."

Even though he's not willing to admit much about himself, Kamkar is willing to share many of his secrets. He has a web site where he actually posts the code he creates so others can replicate his work. What little is known of his background is that Kamkar once formed a company called Fonality and raised $24 million in venture capital for it when he was just 17 years old. Yet he apparently lost all that when he created the Samy worm and crashed MySpace.

One thing is certain though; Samy Kamkar's crusade for privacy and average computer users will continue. The master hacker is passionate about privacy and is willing to fight for it. Samy Kamkar is not only one of the most effective hackers, he is also among the most heroic, sacrificing fame and fortune in order to protect the rights of average people.

Bibliography

BBC News. "Web attack knows where you live." 3 August 2010. bbc.co.uk. BBC News Feature. 4 June 2013.

Houston, Thomas. "Google's Wi-Fi Database May Know Your Router's Physical Location." 25 April 2011. huffingtonpost.com. Huffington Post Feature Article. 4 June 2013.

Kamkar, Samy. "samy.pl." n.d. samy.pl. Personal Website. 4 June 2013.

Vega, Tanzina. "New Web Code Draws Concern Over Privacy Risks." 10 October 2010. nytimes.com. New York Times Feature Article. 4 June 2013.

Wikipedia. "Samy Kamkar." n.d. en.wikipedia.org. Online Encyclopedia Entry. 4 June 2013.